Open Book

Jennifer Tilley

Presentation by *BookLeaf Publishing*

Web: www.bookleafpub.com

E-mail: info@booklcafpub.com

ISBN: 9789357740203

First edition 2023

ACKNOWLEDGEMENT

Throughout my life, I have had plenty of muses, if you will, for my writing to derive from. However, there are a few people that indeed helped me to get to this moment in my dream. God, with whom I couldn't get through anything without. Mom, I will always look at you as a warrior. Your strength inspires me. I could not have asked for a better parent. You taught me the ways of the world and introduced to me the world of writing. Carisma, you are the one that made me a mom and made me see life through a different view. Without you, there is no me. Jessy, the most beautiful heart I have met. Your laughter brightens my day and I am so happy to have you on this journey with me. Megan, your motivational words helped push me to continue on when I didn't feel I could. Marisol, your soul is unmatched. You are such an amazing woman and I am so proud to call you my Friend. Last, but certainly not least, the one person that pushed me to my limit and made this moment happen and a muse for a few of the pieces in here, Remy. I honestly don't know how life functioned before you entered my world. You are my Best Friend and I am so grateful to you for making me push across this "goal line." We are about to Level Up!

I want to Thank You all with everything I have in me. Without this astounding group behind me, I wouldn't be here now, seeing MY WORDS reach the hands of others. I am honored to have you all in my life. Here's to you!

Moment

It's nice.
  What is?

You are.
This.
  Here.
    Now.

Blessed

2

GOD blessed me on a journey,
on a quest,
A never-ending road.
HE blessed me with faith,
with love,
with peace to grow.
HE blessed the path I travel,
this trail,
This one way track.
HE blessed me with joy,
with life,
with courage to not look back.
HE blessed the waters I swam,
the bridges I crossed,
the skies I flew.
GOD blessed me on a journey,
That led me straight to you.

Be Careful, I Will.

So many words to describe,
Whatever this may be.
However, the best one is,
An unexpected blessing.

Our random conversations,
Lead to more somehow.
We try to live in the moment,
Remember, be here now.

The words seem to flow,
Flow so easily from me.
It has become something,
That's done so effortlessly.

It's a daily occurrence,
Talking for hours on end.
We have become somewhat close,
And dare I say, maybe almost friends?

I can be an open book,
Which is easy ammo.
But we keep things between us,
For this, I know.

Learning to just stop,
Taking a moment to smell the roses.
It's true what they say,
One door opens, as another closes.

Watching for the numbers,
And making a wish.
Is something we look forward to,
It's something we can't miss.

You have me learning new things,
With all the talking and the reading.
My mind is so full,
A mosaic filled with meaning.

I know I worry and overthink,
I'm working on that still.
Just remember to always, "Be careful,"
Because "I will."

I can't think of anyone else,
To explore our mind's odyssey.
I guess that you can say,
You're my remedy.

Written Louder

5

I put my words into writing because it seems as
though it is
    Louder.
I can look at you with these green eyes and
express my soul and yet,
you look at me as if you never really know.
You never understand or put the pieces together
and we are left here wondering whether...
    This is all even worth it anymore.

    So,
        I write to you.
Do you see the dots, the ones over the i and the
line that crosses every t? Do you see...
See the curves of the s and the swoop of my y's?
Like the curves of my smile, that has been
unseen for awhile...
But the y,
    the y
    The why...
The sweetest of sorrows left upon the lips.
    The why.
The saddest of whispers seeping through the
ears.
    The why.

The, "How did we get to where we are?" The,
"Why did it have to happen as such?"

      And still,
          Be still.

Let the tear roll down the pale mountain that is
your cheek and you weep. You let it out, while
holding it all in. Its like a tug-of-war inside of
your soul
    You know.
So, I sit and I write to you. Because my words
are louder
    When they are written.

Misplaced

Have you seen it?
I could really use some right now.
You know... That sparkle.
That twinkle in the eye.
    The happiness, that "Wow!"
I seemed to have lost it or at the very least,
misplaced it...
I'm not quite sure how to go about replacing
something...
Something I don't know where it comes from
or even where it goes.
Its there and then its not,
But that's the norm,
    I suppose.
I want that smirk,
with the beating of the heart.
That feeling that you feel,
When your world's not torn apart.
Can you even see it anymore?
I don't feel like it shows,
well, not the way it did before.
Day and night, night and day...
What are we waiting for anyway?
Here I go again huh?
The not-so-peppy posts,

I guess I shouldn't be so verbal,
shouldn't talk about my inner ghosts.
Some say a picture is worth a thousand words,
I guess that could be true...
But looking at the girl in mine,

She hasn't got much to say to you.

Happiest Memories?

I've heard that 'Home is where the happiest
memories are made'...
That's odd because I look around my home and I
feel
    Sad.
I feel like I'm in another person's home. I don't
feel happy.
My memories are
   Painful,
      Unapologetically painful.
The walls are stained with
  Loss,
   With Anger,
    With Unhappy Tears.
The floors are tiled with pieces of broken souls.
The air is turned to a toxic mixture of
  Crying,
   Yelling,
    Dying Laughter.
The foundation is built on
  A Lost Love,
   Misplaced Trust
     and
    Aching Hearts.

Home is where memories are indeed made, but
not happy ones.
The photos that remain are those from a time in
which these memories have been erased. A past
I'm no longer able to grasp, let alone relive.
So much has happened here that you can feel the
tainted loves of the life that it once held. You
walk in as one person and leave as a shell of
who you were. The aura is not of a pleasant past,
but of a time when people tried to be happy.
Grabbing every little smirk that their broken
dreams could get a hold of.
My home does have memories, a lot of them...

But they are far from the happiest of memories,
but rather the...
     Unhappiest.

My Crown

My crown has fallen,
Right onto the floor.
I no longer have enough,
To hold it up anymore.

It's been tarnished,
By the uneasy years.
From the aches and pains,
And the burden of tears.

I carried it high,
I've carried it long.
But to keep my head up?
I'm no longer strong.

It is bent up,
Damn near broken.
With thoughts,
That can no longer be spoken.

The jewels have scattered,
Have all been misplaced.
From every scar,
From every mistake.

Everything has slipped,
Right from my hand.
I held on too tight,
Like a fist full of sand.

The road is long,
But the journey much longer.
I've done all I can,
But, it is I, who is conquered.

My heart remains beating,
For the mere reason of living.
But if you must know,
I'm tired of giving.

I've loved all I can,
Gave to some not worthy.
But the crown I so cherished,
No longer suits me.

The words I speak,
Will remain in this prison.
But silence speaks louder,
For those that will listen.

Scarred

I've been through a lot. I've seen a lot. Felt a lot.
I have been put through the ringer and beyond.
I've had things happen, things that some cannot
begin to fathom.
    But I'm still here.
My guard is tough, my wall is strong. If I let you
in, it's because i see something in you that brings
out something in
me.
See, I take every scenario into account. Both
good and bad. I look into your eyes and I
calculate a list of pros and cons, which you
never even know about and I...
    Test the waters.
I burn easily though.
I think too much and I tend to sabotage myself.
My relationships. My...
    Happiness.
But be patient. Please be patient, for I fear the
worst of many situations and my conclusions are
sometimes far off. My judgement isn't always
clear and I can be a bit Jaded.
Hard.
Stubborn.
Insecure.

I feel unworthy 8 times out of 10 and I'll
question you. Boy, oh boy, will I ever question
you! Never to your face though. But I promise
you that you have made so many excuses in my
head that I'll be angry at you for
   'No
      Apparent
         Reason'
I'm sorry for that. I'm sorry for neglecting your
ability to tell me your side, your truth. The
REAL truth.
So please be kind.
Please be strong.
Please be patient.
     I
    Am
    Scarred.

Three Hearts

Pressed ever so lightly,
Against my chest.
The beating becomes one,
As we quietly rest.
You never made a word,
Not a peep, nor a cry.
You didn't even appear,
Before I had to say goodbye.
Three Hearts,
Each one a different beat.
With your own set of eyes,
And your own little feet.
I never got to see you,
Nor hold you in my arms.
I didn't get to hear you,
Not your wisdom or your charm.
Three Hearts,
Nestled here upon my chest.
The metal that portrays you,
Will remain second best.
Imagination runs rampant,
In the stillness of my mind.
Trying to see it all play out,
I feel like I'm completely blind.
I cannot see your faces,

I cannot see your clothes.
I see figures running,
That's as far as the scene goes.
Three Hearts,
Representing those I never met.
To secretly remind me,
So I can never forget.

My Heart is a Diary

My heart is a diary.
It's steady taking notes.
You would be shocked to hear,
Some of the things she has wrote.
Flirting with tragedy,
For as long as she's written.
Waiting for the fall,
Feeling cold, almost frostbitten.
Anticipating the shatter,
Before it even begins.
Once she has her sights set,
She's preparing for the end.
Self sabotage is her nature,
It's her state of mind.
Always ready for the letdown,
Whilst waiting for the climb.
My heart is a diary.
A bit tattered and frayed.
From those that left too soon,
And those that overstayed.
Never finding the balance,
To keep from tipping over.
Feeling a bit shaky,
She's never quite sober.
Drinking in all she can,

From everyone that she crosses.
She holds on to their memory,
While tallying up the losses.
Wishing she can go back,
To where she began.
To keep herself from falling,
Into another's hand.
She works rather hard,
To keep herself true.
But she never encountered,
Someone with the likes of you.
You're holding her gently,
Yet firmly, so still.
Tending to her cuts,
Making sure she isn't ill.
She takes her pen,
Slowly jots this down.
She can't believe what she's writing,
Or fathom what she's found.
My diary is left open,
From beginning to end.
He reads it ever so softly,
With a subtle grin.
He touches where she lies,
Just beneath the bone,
My heart is a diary,
And she has finally found home.

Guru

What are words?
  When thoughts are rampant.
What are thoughts?
  When eyes are windows.
What are eyes?
  When hearts speak volumes.
What are hearts?
    When souls are boundless.

Become one with the outside.
Become one with your self.
Learning who you are,
Is a journey, intensely felt.
The teacher will teach,
And guru will lead.
Explore your inner path,
And words you'll no longer need.
Sit in the silence,
Breathe your true self in.
Shed the negativity you hold,
Releasing of your physical skin.
Allow the world to slip,
Slip from consciousness,
Forget all you may know,

You'll thank me for this.
Meditate on the present,
For this can reveal...
All you can learn,
And how to truly heal.
The spirit will relax,
Be in harmony alone.
The burdens you carry,
No longer heavy as stone.
Learn to be comfortable,
Being alone and in silence.
You don't need anyone,
Being your soul's hindrance.
For what we may think,
Is honest and true.
May be the very thing,
That's destroying you.
Remember to always,
Seek for knowledge and growth.
For your eternal life,
Has taken an oath.
Never be persuaded,
By those that don't believe.
The spirit knows exactly,
Where you need to be.

The Red That Paints His Fury

He towers over her,
Breath heavy yet steady.
The thin, cold metal pressed against her,
She knows that he's ready.
The build up took years,
But happened in the blink of an eye.
She cannot begin to understand,
What happened to this guy.
His smiles and love,
Disingenuous at best.
She gave all she had,
And yet, he still took the rest.
The world was his stage,
Which he performed on so well.
When little did they know,
He was the keeper of hell.
She couldn't fathom,
How it all came to this.
Was it something she said?
Were there signs that she missed?
She should have said yes,
She should have caved in.
She should have succumbed,
To what he wanted then.
Her pleading falls,

On silent eyes and ears.
The red that paints his fury,
Was fueled by her tears.
The years that passed,
Seemed to dissolve into the abyss,
She was finally ready,
It was enough of this!
She walked away,
With a baby in her arms.
She was no longer phased,
By his unhinged charm.
The memories do remain,
They stay buried in her mind.
Recovery is possible,
But it will take some time.
One day turns into a month,
One week into a year.
No longer despising her reflection,
She no longer hates the mirror.
Looking back on that time,
She wasn't as weak as she felt.
She simply was rearranging,
The cards she'd been dealt.
Today, she stands tall,
Strong in her own will.
She is cut from a different cloth,
Made with a guard of steel.
Never returning,
To that dark place inside.

She's moved on to better,
With strength she no longer hides.

23

The Midnight Shore

The salty aroma that washes over me,
   The calmness hits almost immediately.
No malice, no anger, no hate,
   Steadily washing the raw feelings away.
Let me swim away with the sea,
   For the water doesn't think the worst of me.
The push and pull, almost a tug-of-war,
   Crashing upon the midnight shore.
The ocean knows nothing of your past,
   It simply flows as time isn't grasped.
Take me away, let me float in the sea,
   Allow the water to wash over me.
No imperfections, nothing to prove,
   Feeling the current beneath me move.
I want to feel the weight on my shoulders,
   Be flushed away as the waves grow colder.
The ocean doesn't know what I have done,
   It has no record of the pain I've numbed.
Slowly slipping into its depths,
   I belong to the waves I've come to accept.
I want to run away with the fish in the sea,
   For the water, is the only true love for me.

Hi(gh)

From the very first moment,
That very first hi(gh),
Watching the curve of your smile,
It surely caught my eye.
Every meeting that passed,
Made me wonder a little more.
Was I feeling good because of you,
Or simply from the score?
Time steadily passed by,
As things began to change.
We grew closer together,
It never felt strange.
We have the same theories,
Think of things in the same way.
We can talk about anything,
At any time, night or day.
I never would have thought,
Talking to you would just flow.
Like the clouds that line the sky,
Or the sun that shines below.
That pep in your step,
As you walk up to greet me.
Always makes me giggle,
And makes me all giddy.
The foundation we have built,

Has taken some time.
I could not have foreseen this,
Blooming from that first hi(gh).

Perpetual Cycle

Inconsiderate, grief is.
The incessant gnawing away at pieces of you.
Your heart
	cement, stonelike, archaic.

	The spirit, broken.

We spend our days trying to placate ourselves
with promises,
				"It was their time."
				"It'll get better."
			"Time will heal your pain."

We spend our days ambivalent about life.
Making the same egregious mistake of thinking
time will heal us.
	It doesn't.

It simply dulls the point in which we are
repeatedly stabbed with.
	The not so subtle reminder that you aren't here
anymore.
The not so subtle reminder that the last time we
saw you was…
	The LAST time we saw you.

Humans have a plethora of emotions and yet…
grief.
  It flows. Like the waves of the ocean.
The waves crash into you.
The waves crash into you.
  The waves… At times, almost drowning.

Grief holds the most bewitching stare.
The kind of stare that takes your breath away.
The kind of stare that makes you feel like the
world disappeared.
The kind of stare that depletes your energy.
The kind of stare that removes your identity.

One day, you think about it less. It's still there,
lurking. Waiting.
  You feel, if you dare to say, okay. Your
breathing doesn't feel labored.
You can feel the sun today. You can feel the
wind today.
You can hear her laugh and smell his cologne.
  The rush of pain washes over you.

The waves are back. They always come back.
You can't fight them.
  So, you succumb to this perpetual cycle. It
never ends.
Inconsiderate, grief is.

In Loving Memory of

Sylvia Valdez Ibarra
(7/1/69 - 10/16/21)
&
Juan Francisco Cardenas Medina
(10/5/70 - 12/31/21)

*Not a day goes by where grief isn't a friend of
mine.

You Are...

30

You are the answer,

to the question,

that I haven't asked.

You are the dream,

in my sleep,

before I close my eyes.

You are the future,

to the past,

that I haven't lived.

You are the sadness,

in my voice,

before I could miss you.

You are the song,

to the melody,

that I haven't hummed.

You are the tear,

in my eye,

before I could smile.

You are the idea,

in my head,

that I haven't thought.

You are the jump,

in my step,

before I could walk.

You are the butterfly,

in my stomach,

before we first kissed.

You are the love,

in my heart,

that I haven't felt.

You are the need,

in my life,

before I could live.

You are the I,

in me,

that I haven't found.

Sabotage

The words that replay in my head,
    Are not kind.
I feel them creeping up. Almost out of nowhere.
They tell me things. They make me visualize the
worst.
They make me feel like I'm the worst.
I feel alone.
    They say I should be alone. That is all I am
good for after all.
Then, I see this ray of sunshine. This smile that
shines so bright.
I fight the words in my head.
The broken record that is my past.
The broken record of all the negative people that
tore me down.
This sunshine rips through and I feel some sort
of… peace.
The words subside for a while and I feel a smile.
Not the type of smile that I use to mask the
sadness.
Not the type of smile that fools the world.
A real, genuine smile. A smile that feels
heavenly.
Then, one day, the strength of this smile
It is not as strong as the day before

And the words sneak back in.
My nails begin to be bitten on. My skin picked
at.
I bleed.
The itchy feeling beneath my skin comes and I
scratch.
I feel the anxious pit in my stomach and I
become consumed by this.
I cannot fight back. The words.
The words. The words.
They surround me.
I shake. I cry. I lose.
I let all the good go… I lose.
I sabotage all that is best for me… Why?
The words, of course.
   They are the only ones that have been by my
side all this time.
They have always been there for me. How could
I let them down now?

Hopeless

35

Should be asleep right now.
Yet, here I am.
 Awake. Thinking.
 Not really sure what to do now.
How to react. What is going to happen?
Granted, it could be so much worse
 I know that.

But when I'm in this moment of disbelief, hurt,
pain....
Loneliness,
It's hard to see anything else but that.
It's difficult to focus on what few good things I
have left.

Yes, I smile, I joke,
 Even laugh til I can't breathe.
But I also remain quiet, break down
 And cry til I can't breathe.
Life has ups && downs, I know that.
 You know that.
 We all know that.
 But lately... My
 d
 o

w
n
S

are far more visible than my ups.

In fact, they are at a steady pace. Making me
feel less than I am, unworthy of certain things,
certain people.
I'm desperately looking for that one ray of hope,
in what seems to be a...
Hopeless place.
Yes, I can be dramatic... Believe me, I know.
But as I've said, "I cannot see past this moment."
Cannot view the possibility of it getting any
better right now. I'm not saying it never will,
cause I have seen it before, but right now it's...

Unfathomable.

Jennifer.

I'm difficult,
but my heart is like no other.
I'm different,
but you'll never find another.
I curse like a sailor,
but pray to no end.
I'm too blunt at times,
but I'll be your best friend.
I'm honest,
sometimes to a fault.
I tell it like it is,
But it's not an assault.
Some say I'm pessimistic,
but that's not what I say.
I'm merely realistic,
The let downs are easier that way.
I look for love in all the wrong places,
but I yearn for the look of happiness on their
faces.
I have been beaten,
I've been used.
I've been left on my own,
mentally and emotionally bruised.
I've had my ups,
and I've had my downs.

But when it comes to me,
I seem to always stick around.
Maybe one day,
I can have what others do.
The one to call my own,
That is honest and true.
My heart is tattered,
it's as fragile as can be.
But maybe, just maybe…
he'll love me for me.

Carisma

I'm sorry that you had to witness,
So many negative things.
You saw some of the worst,
Before you were even a teen.
I tried to shield your eyes,
Your ears and even your heart.
I know I failed in that,
Because I've seen you fall apart.
You never express your feelings,
You're a pro at holding them in.
It's something I wish I worked on with you,
So you didn't have such thick skin.
You build up a wall,
A guard, even against me.
I feel like I missed the time,
To be a better "mommy."
We don't see eye to eye,
It's hard to communicate,
I want to fix these issues,
But I'm afraid it may be too late.
I can see the hurt,
Hidden in your beautiful brown eyes,
I want to do better by you,
I really hate to see you cry.
I am sorry I haven't been the best,

I am trying, to no avail.
I have never given up on us,
We have not been derailed.
Working on us,
Is my number one goal,
I want us to be closer,
Even when I'm gray and old.
I know it won't be easy,
But I have faith that we can do it.
I have always wondered,
Why was I chosen to do this?
Being a single parent,
Is a hard job, no doubt.
But, Carisma, my baby girl,
You're the one I can't live without.
This is definitely something that I,
I never fully imagined.
That one day I could have,
A Mini-Me Best Friend.

Letter

Hey,

 its nice to see you again. Im sorry I haven't been around a lot in the past. I feel like I have missed out on so much and I haven't been the best friend to you...
I'm sorry to hear about the pain and heartbreak you had felt. I know I wasn't there to work through it all with you and I know that is my fault. I'm not sure why I tend to disappear at the times you need me the most. I don't mean to and I don't really have an excuse. It just

 Happens.
Sometimes, I just feel so small that I don't matter much. I am working on that cause I know it's just something that goes on in my head. I have seen you go completely numb when certain things happen and I wish I could help, but I am not sure what to say to make it all better. I feel like I make things worse... Im sure you understand that too.
We have so much to talk about, so much to see and explore together and so much to fix. When we are both free,

 of course.

I am going to try to be more present in your life
and in the lives of others. I really don't want you
to forget who I am.

But we have to focus on it together.
Hey, just do me a favor, yeah?... Let's not be
strangers anymore, ok? I'll see you soon.

To Me.
        Love,
                Me.

www.ingramcontent.com/pod-product-compliance
Lightning Source LLC
LaVergne TN
LVHW021307200726

843509LV00012B/1826